Overcome Anxiety and End Your Suffering Now

Written by: <u>Beau Norton</u>

CEO & Founder of
Health & Happiness Foundation

Go to <u>healthandhappinessfoundation.com</u>
for your free personal development tips
and tools.

My Free Gift to You

To help speed up your personal transformation, I have made an affirmation audio track that you can listen to at your convenience. This mp3 uses binaural beat technology, which helps the suggestions penetrate the depths of your subconscious mind where they will begin to shift your beliefs to ones that will better serve you on your journey.

If you are interested, go to the following web address to get your copy:

healthandhappinessfoundation.com/101-affirmations-for-success-audio

Introduction: You Can Change

Let me tell you a little about my journey. Back in 2011, I was a freshman in college, and I was absolutely miserable. I was failing my classes, 40 pounds overweight (something quite new for me), and my girlfriend of a year and a half had just broken up with me. I had severe social anxiety, so I had almost no social life whatsoever, and I was in the midst of a deep, dark depression that left me wallowing in sorrow and self-pity practically 24/7. Most days, I couldn't even muster the willpower to get out of bed. I drowned my sorrows by drinking alcohol 3 nights a week and eating fast food 2-3 times per day. I was in a vicious downward spiral. It was sink or swim for me. I decided to swim, and here I am writing this, happy as ever, in an attempt to share with you my knowledge on what it takes to overcome depression. First of all, I want to let you know that no matter where you stand at this moment, *you can change*. You can live your dreams and go on to do amazing things in the world. If you are reading this, then you are on the right track.

This book is going to provide you with multiple strategies and tips that you can use to steadily climb from the pits of depression to the heights of happiness. I can't tell you it will be easy, but I can assure you it's worth it. Everything you want is only a decision away. If you commit to your own growth and vow to never give up, then you will do extraordinary things and be an inspiration to many. If you lack belief in your ability to overcome your depression, then that's okay, because this book will provide you with the hope and inspiration that you need. I'm here to offer you a helping hand, because I know that none of us can do it alone. My love goes out to you. I know you will make it through this. Let's explore what it's going to take, shall we?

Internal vs. External

From experience, I'm convinced that depression is completely internal, however, external factors can play a huge role in determining your inner environment (thoughts and attitudes). It's very easy to place the blame on these external circumstances, but it should be avoided at all costs. Instead, you need to take complete responsibility for your current circumstances and realize that you have unconsciously created them. You may not have wished for them, but through a series of thoughts and decisions, you have brought them into your life. This means you are also responsible for changing them if that's what you desire.

Some external things that may be having a negative impact on you could be family, friends, your job, the television shows you watch, the music you listen to, the food you eat, or the cleanliness of your home. The list could go on and on, but these are some of the major things you should be aware of. I will go into a few in more detail later on, but for the moment I just want you to take a look at your life from an objective viewpoint and try to see whether some of the above things might be holding you back. Perhaps your job is stressful and you don't enjoy it at all, or maybe you have the tendency to watch very violent movies and TV shows. Maybe you have friends or family that aren't very supportive of you, or maybe your home is a mess and just looking at it makes you feel bad. Whatever it is, it's important that you admit to yourself that some things need changing. Don't worry about changing anything right now. Simply being aware of the problem is enough. Awareness is the foundation of positive change. When you start being honest with yourself and begin to notice the areas of your life that are causing you negative emotions, your life will naturally begin to improve. Denial guarantees stagnation. Awareness guarantees growth.

When I began my personal journey of self-development, the first major thing that changed was my circle of friends. I stopped hanging out with a lot of the people I was once close with. It happened all by itself without me having to think too much about it. I was improving myself so quickly that old friends naturally got left behind. We just no longer had as much in common. I was focused on becoming successful and happy, while they were still doing the same things they had been doing for years. I understood that I could not afford to surround myself with people that didn't have similar goals. It was nothing against them, but I just knew the importance of putting myself in the best environment possible. They say you become like the 5 people you spend the most time with, and I have found that to be absolutely true.

I'm telling you this because from my experience, I've come to see that the number one thing that holds people back from achieving their goals and getting on the path to a better life is their circle of friends. The hard truth is that you will most likely have to cut some people out of your life if you want better things for yourself. You cannot afford to surround yourself with negative people if you want to live a positive life. If you are lucky, then you might have some very supportive and encouraging friends. Keep those people close, but consider eliminating or drastically reducing the amount of time you spend with the people who aren't happy or doing much with their lives. You will become like the people you spend time with. Their habits and tendencies will rub off on you very quickly. On my journey, I've spent a lot of time alone for this very reason. It's always a better idea to be alone than to be with negative people. And being alone gives you a great opportunity to learn how to love yourself more, which is crucial for living a happy and fulfilling life.

Everything from your external environment that you allow to enter your mind and body becomes part of your internal environment. Memories get stored, energy gets absorbed, and attitudes get engrained in your mind. Everything from your place of employment to the type of music you listen to has an impact on your thoughts and attitudes. Considering that your thoughts determine the quality of your life and your level of happiness, you would be wise to reevaluate your life and determine what is serving you and what is not. If something doesn't feel right or makes you feel bad, then it should be avoided. This process takes time and requires awareness, but it will have a major impact on your life.

Becoming aware of your external environment is important, but I believe that consciously shaping your life from the inside out is far more powerful. Since your thoughts have led to the decisions that got you to where you are today, focusing on improving your thoughts will ensure you end up in a better place than you are right now. People have the tendency to think that everything happens "out there," when in reality it all happens "in here." Change your thoughts, change your life. You will find that your external environment automatically changes as your internal environment changes. I have seen this to be true for myself, and I have studied countless other successful people who all say the same thing. Change starts from within. This doesn't mean to neglect making changes to your external environment. It means that the majority of your time spent improving yourself should be focused within. The next chapter will explain exactly how to mold your inner environment for maximum success and happiness.

Awareness: The Foundation of Positive Change

For someone who is depressed, introspection and self-analysis is a must. There is often the tendency to want to avoid problems and repress emotions out of a fear of coming face to face with them, but this must be avoided at all costs. You must be willing to face your inner demons to have any chance of ridding yourself of them. The more you avoid them, the deeper and deeper they go and the harder they become to eliminate.

Repressed emotions actually affect the body in very noticeable ways. They cause tension in the muscles, which can lead to chronic stress, high blood pressure, headaches, severe anxiety, and disease. It is crucial that you muster the courage to go within and face the underlying causes of your current condition. It can be scary, but it is absolutely necessary. It's not so bad when you realize that *you are not your thoughts*. You are just the temporary owner of thoughts, and that means you control your thoughts and not the other way around. Having negative thoughts does not mean you are a bad person. It only means that you have temporarily lost touch with who you really are. And who you really are is someone far greater than you currently believe. Underneath all those negative thoughts is a beautiful person with unlimited potential. You may not see it now, but I promise that you will once you overcome this and learn how to be happy again.

As I mentioned, when I was in the process of overcoming my severe depression years ago, I spent a lot of time alone. I'm an introvert by nature, so it was what I preferred. If you are an introvert, then you have a slight advantage. Although I believe introverts are more susceptible to depression, I think they are also more likely to overcome it. Overcoming depression requires a lot of introspection and self-analysis, which introverts do naturally, so they tend to work through their problems much quicker. Extroverted people tend to look "out there" for answers, not realizing that their problem lies within. Due to the nature of extroverted people, they may have more trouble solving inner conflicts. At the same time, they are really good at temporarily forgetting their problems due to their social and outgoing nature. Introverts will often sit around and stew in their negative emotions, leading them into a downward spiral. Both have their advantages and pitfalls, but the real message that I wish to convey by telling you this is the importance of facing your problems rather than avoiding them. And by that I mean looking within yourself. You may believe your problems lie out in the world somewhere, but you will never be able to create lasting change in your life unless you first change yourself from the inside. You may be able to temporarily patch up a broken relationship, but if you didn't do any of the necessary inner work, the same problems will eventually surface again. You may be able to get some happiness by changing jobs, but that happiness won't last if you didn't change your inner environment, that is your thoughts and your attitudes toward life. You can move to the most beautiful place in the world, but you still have to take your mind and body with you. If you don't learn to go within and change your thoughts, then nothing will change.

If you are reading this book, then you are already aware that something in your life needs to change. It's a good sign that you are reading this, because that means you have come to accept some responsibility for your current situation. Some people just have too much pride to admit that they need to change. Fortunately, that is not you. Now all you need to do is go a little deeper and try to uncover the root cause of your depression. You may already have a good idea, but it's important that you get as specific as possible, because that will allow you to re-contextualize things and see them in a more positive light. The next section will describe a simple process for you to uncover the hidden blocks that are preventing you from living the life you desire.

Introspection and Analysis

It's likely that you already have a general idea of what is causing your depression, or at least you think you do. In my case years ago, one might say that I became depressed because my girlfriend broke up with me, I was overweight, and was failing college. This is where people make a huge mistake. They blame external events, when really the cause of depression lies within. In my case, the actual cause of my depression was not those seemingly negative events and circumstances but rather my reaction and interpretation of them. Since I had very low self-esteem at the time and was not very mentally or emotionally strong, I was extremely prone to depression, anxiety, and other mental/emotional issues. Going out and getting another girlfriend was not going to solve anything. It might have temporarily boosted my self-esteem, but if my next girlfriend happened to break up with me, I would be a complete mess just like the first time. The only way for me to really solve anything was to go inside and determine the thoughts and attitudes that were controlling my reactions and interpretations of events and circumstances. Because I delved within, I was able to create permanent and lasting change rather than just a quick fix. The following describes the exact process that I used to uncover the hidden cause of my depression.

I knew that the problem was with my thoughts, so my main objective was to discover the specific thoughts that were the cause of my suffering. I knew that once I found them, I could begin to let them go and replace them with more positive thoughts that served me much better. Just by the way I felt, I could tell that my thoughts were of a very demeaning and self-critical nature. I did not respect myself and had very low self-esteem. I was lucky enough to know that the unfortunate circumstances of my life at the time were the result of my dominant thoughts and not the other way around, so I was determined to change myself from the inside out.

The way I began was with creative self-expression through poetry. Poetry allowed me to express my thoughts in a creative way that I could actually feel proud of. Even though my thoughts were mostly negative, I didn't feel so bad about them when I could express them as art. It was very healing for me to get my thoughts out onto paper. It was the only thing that made me genuinely happy at that point in my life. I strongly believe that every person who is going through a depression can benefit greatly from expressing themselves through writing. The process of writing itself is healing, but what makes writing extremely powerful is the fact that it creates awareness. Writing out your thoughts allows you to see them for what they really are–*just thoughts*. When those thoughts are out of your head, you suddenly no longer identify with them in the same way you once did. Instead of judging and condemning yourself for your awful thoughts, you realize that they are just words, and *words can be changed*.

I encourage you to begin a journaling practice immediately. Freehand write for at least 10 minutes per day without editing or censoring yourself. Write exactly what comes to mind. Spill your guts. No one is going to read it but you, so be completely honest with yourself and let all your deepest, darkest thoughts rise to the surface. From there, they can be released onto paper through the pen in your hand, and you will be freed of one burden at a time. I encourage everyone to write in a journal on a daily basis, but you especially need to if you are depressed or struggling with negative emotions. It's amazing to watch the transformation that takes place just from this one simple practice. Start today. If it helps, get a nice leather bound journal or something colorful that is pleasing for you to look at. Get excited about it! This is your life after all, and this is one step towards a brighter future.

Journaling itself is powerful, but I have a few tips that will help you to make it even more transformative. Once you have written your entry for the day, re-read what you have written and try to point out any negative thoughts you may have written down. Choose one and re-write it at the bottom of the page. Then, you are going to re-frame that statement to make it positive. This is how you will turn yourself from a pessimist to an optimist, a negative thinker to a positive one, and that will make ALL the difference in your life. For example, let's say you had a bad day and wrote, "Nothing went well for me today. I feel like everyone is against me and nothing ever works out how I want it to." Once you have written this at the bottom of the page, put a light X through it, and then below it write something like, "Today might have been a bad day, but I know that brighter days lie ahead. My future is bright and I won't let one bad day ruin my mood." Circle this statement. You have successful reframed a negative into a positive, and you are now one step closer to becoming the happy, upbeat, passionate person you desire to be.

You see, you always have the choice of how you want to look at things. A negative situation is only negative in the eyes of the person who chooses to see it that way. You can always choose to turn a negative into a positive. It takes practice, but it is well worth the initial effort, because positive thoughts bring positive results. Your happiness is directly correlated with the amount of positive thoughts that you think. To beat your depression fast and experience greater amounts of happiness, your main objective should always be to look at the things in your life in a more positive light. Truth is subjective. A tragedy to one can be a blessing to another. It's not about the situation itself but rather your perception of it.

How can we realistically deal with the seemingly 'negative' events that are an inevitable part of life? People die, relationships end, jobs get lost, cars break down, and a whole slew of other events that most people view as 'bad' or 'unfortunate.' I have a simple solution:

always look for the lesson. All 'negative' events hold a hidden lesson and a buried treasure. Most people's immediate reaction to unfortunate events is to say, "Oh, how awful" or "What a tragedy." Most people automatically look for the problem rather than the solution. I'll tell you one thing: life is much more beautiful when you look for the good in all, and that is always nothing more than a matter of choice. You may be automatically conditioned to look for the tragedy rather than the lesson behind the tragedy, but that's quite normal and it's exactly why I have taught you this journaling exercise. Start reframing your own negative thoughts into positive thoughts, and your whole world will slowly start to brighten. When you make positive thinking a habit, life tends to start working out in your favor. Even when it doesn't, you will be looking for the beauty, and so you will find it.

When in the midst of a depression, it can be very difficult to find the lesson in it. You probably won't immediately see the incredible blessing that it is, but I encourage you to start looking for the positives. My own depression was my greatest blessing, because it caused me to focus on bettering myself. If it wasn't for my depression, I would probably still be living a mediocre life. I didn't see how my depression was a blessing until over a year after it ended, but today it is very clear to me. Tears of joy and gratitude often roll down my cheeks when I stop to think of all the struggles I've overcome. I promise you that you will look back on your current struggle and feel exactly the same. The lesson may be hidden at the moment, but your job is to uncover it and turn this struggle into a stepping stone for your great achievements to come.

In the early stages of introspection and self-analysis, a lot of negative thoughts and emotions will be coming to the surface. This may be uncomfortable, but it is absolutely necessary for your personal growth. Commit to writing in a journal on a daily basis, and you will see massive progress over time. Having the honesty to admit the presence of negative and harmful thoughts is a huge step in and of itself. You have transcended the stage of denial and victimhood and moved into courage and responsibility. At this stage, your recovery is essentially guaranteed. The speed at which you recover will depend on your ability to surrender your problems and choose a more positive focus. The whole process will be much easier if you can come to a level of understanding and acceptance. I will cover this in more detail in the following section.

Acceptance: Surrendering Your Problems

The next major step is acceptance. Accept that you are here for reason, and that every challenge is nothing more than a stepping stone to your brighter future. You don't enjoy your suffering, but you accept it because you really have no other choice. Resisting it will only ensure its survival. What you resist persists. Therefore, acceptance is a crucial step in the process of transcending negativity and rising to a level of joy and fulfillment. Understand that you are not your thoughts and that you can change them and dramatically change your life in the process. You are not stuck where you are. Make the decision right now to move forward at all costs. Never resign yourself to suffering. Commit to growth, and you will grow. Commit to overcoming this, and you will.

Acceptance will allow you to overcome negativity and move you to a place of neutrality. From a neutral position, you can begin consciously shaping your life by making rational rather than emotional decisions. At a level of negativity, making bad decisions that have negative consequences is very common, because decisions at this level often result from emotional positions that are not based on rational thinking or morality. At the level of negativity, it is easy to get trapped in a vicious cycle of bad decisions based on poor judgement that lead to negative consequences, thus reinforcing the negative attitude. This is why it is of utmost importance that you move from negativity to neutrality, and the easiest path is through acceptance.

Acceptance comes through understanding rather than judgement. The most basic thing that needs to be understood is the fact that you have created your current circumstances *unconsciously*. No one consciously chooses to be depressed. You can begin to accept your past mistakes by coming to the realization that you did the best you could with what you knew at the time. If you could have done any better, you would have. All you can work with is the present moment, and the best thing you could do right now is *forgive yourself*. Your mistakes have brought you to this moment so you could learn, and so they were actually a blessing! If you didn't mess up somewhere along the journey, you would have nothing to guide you in the right direction. Forgive yourself and accept that you are here for a very good reason.

Through your introspection and self-analysis, you will become very aware of your negative thoughts. Self-doubt, criticism, judgement, guilt, and resentment will come to the surface, and it may feel very uncomfortable, but remember that it is only surfacing so that it can be resolved. In the past, you probably weren't very aware of the specific thoughts that were causing your negative emotions, and so you have most likely been placing a lot of blame on yourself. When you become more aware, you will no longer feel the need to be so hard on yourself. You will see that your thoughts do not actually define you. They occur spontaneously as a result of your past conditioning. But now you are aware of your own thoughts and realize that they can be changed and no longer have to control you. Now you can take back your power and forgive yourself for not being aware in the past. You couldn't change back then because you simply did not have the knowledge and awareness to do so. You can now relax knowing that you can finally exercise maximum control over your life. The next section will teach you how.

Bioenergetic Analysis

Bioenergetics is the study of the body and its relationship with the mind. Specifically, it focuses on releasing tension within the musculature of the body. This tension is caused mostly by repressed memories of childhood traumas. In our early years, we learned to cope with stress by storing energy in our muscles rather than releasing it. As a child, we may have been taught that it was 'bad' to feel angry or sad, so instead of expressing ourselves, we learned to repress our feelings. Of course, this happens unconsciously, but it has a major effect on us well into our adult years. It's very possible that you have a lot of unreleased energy trapped in your body that is inhibiting your ability to feel positive emotions. Feelings such as joy and happiness require the release of energy. For some people, this release is not possible due to massive amounts of tension in their bodies. If you feel stressed a lot of the time, then you have a lot of muscular tension that needs to be released. When you learn to freely express your energy, you will find that depression, anxiety, anger, and other unpleasant emotions naturally disappear and positive emotions such as happiness, joy, and even ecstasy become the norm.

You are likely not even aware of the tension in your body since it has been there since childhood. When you are made conscious of it, however, the tension becomes obvious. For example, almost all people have large amounts of tension in their jaws as a result of not being allowed to express themselves as children. People are often taught to "sit down and shut up" as young children, and this shows up in adulthood as self-consciousness and low self-esteem. These character traits can actually be gradually reversed by simply releasing the tension in the areas of the body associated with that particular tendency. If you feel inhibited in any way, then there is likely large amounts of tension stored in areas of your body such as your jaw, neck, shoulders, back, abdomen, pelvis, and legs. You've probably never been very aware of this tension—until now. Take a few minutes to feel each one of your body parts. Notice any tension. The most obvious places will be your jaw, shoulders, abdomen, and buttocks. Becoming aware is the first step. From there, you can begin to heal yourself.

Releasing Tension Through Self-Expression

Now that you are at least slightly aware of the tension in your body, you can begin to consciously release that tension. This will slowly free you of many negative emotions and make way for the positive ones that you desire.

The body is sometimes referred to in bioenergetics and psychoanalysis as the expression of the subconscious mind. Your depression and unhappiness was not consciously chosen, so it must be a result of the content of your subconscious mind. If this is the case, then wouldn't it make sense to look at the body for clues as to what's going on in your mind? It turns out that this is an extremely effective method for reprogramming the subconscious mind and thus drastically altering the way life is experienced. In the next chapter, I will discuss how to work with the mind more directly, but I think it is important to first discuss how the body is involved in the process. Considering the mind and body are not separate but one, knowledge on how they are connected and how you can use one to affect the other will serve you greatly.

For most of us, our self-expression has been hindered. As a result, we experience stress, anxiety, chronic fatigue, depression, and much more. The solution is to gradually begin expressing ourselves in healthy ways. This can be done in a variety of ways. First, I'll give you a list of expressive activities to consider, and then I will describe a specific method that will benefit you tremendously when done on a daily basis. Here are some simple activities you can begin doing that will gradually reduce the tension in your body and allow you to experience more joy and happiness:

- **Jump on a <u>rebounder</u>.** A rebounder is a mini trampoline that you can use practically anywhere. Jumping on one of these is beneficial for a variety of reasons, but the main benefit is that it massages and relaxes the muscles throughout your body and increases the blood flow to them. Jumping for 10 minutes daily can have a dramatic positive effect on your mood and overall health. Don't believe me? Give it a try. I promise it will change your life.

- **Use a <u>vibration plate</u>.** This is beneficial for the same reasons as the rebounder, but it has an even more powerful effect. A vibration plate is just a platform that you stand on that vibrates your entire body. It is excellent for releasing muscular tension and has many other benefits. After each use, you will feel much more energetic and happy, mainly because it releases tension (emotional blocks) and allows you to express yourself more naturally.

- **Sing, dance, hum, jump around, and be silly whenever possible.** Most of us only do these things when we are alone. This goes to show that we are inhibited in our self-expression. This is mainly due to social and cultural conditioning, but what is even worse is when someone doesn't even express themselves when they are alone. If you are ever alone with no one around, you should use that time to express yourself as much as possible! Your happiness depends on it. Even expressing yourself with no one around to see will have a major impact of how you act in all situations. I wouldn't expect you to bust out dancing in public, but doing so alone will free you from the self-judgement that has been stealing your happiness.

- **Get regular massages or use a foam roller.** Massages are obviously a great way to release tension. I think that more people should treat themselves to massages *at least* once per month. Most people's bodies are so riddled with stress that they would be wise to get them *once per week*. If you can't afford massages that often, you can simply purchase a <u>foam roller</u> and do the job yourself. It is also a wonderful tool for preventing soreness after a workout.

- **Avoid remaining stagnant; get up and express yourself.** When we are depressed, there is the tendency to want to sit around and do a whole lot of *nothing.* Chronic tension inhibits the flow of energy, and so a depressed person invariably has low amounts of motivation. It is crucial that you muster some willpower and move your body on a daily basis. The act of movement itself allows the energy to flow, which gradually lifts you out of your depression. The more you move, the better off you will be. Start an exercise routine, join a dance class, or just take a walk. Movement of any kind will benefit you greatly.

There you have 5 simple ways to relieve tension and thus reduce stress and anxiety caused by muscular tension. When the anxiety dissipates, it makes room for positive emotions to flow through you. Joy is an experience felt *in the body.* Therefore, it is impossible to feel joy if the flow of energy in the body is inhibited by muscular tension as it is in so many people. I encourage you to practice self-expression in whatever form feels most comfortable to you. The worst thing you could do when depressed is sit on the couch and watch television. Express yourself first by perhaps getting some exercise. Relax all you want afterwards. You will actually thoroughly enjoy watching a movie and doing a whole lot of nothing when you know that you got your dose of positive self-expression for the day.

Bioenergetic Breakthrough: The Bow

The Bow is a simple bioenergetic exercise that can greatly reduce tension and emotional blocks. It is effective because it forces the blocked energy in the body to be expressed. The expression is easily noticed in the vibration of the entire body when the exercise is performed. The great thing about *the bow* is that it can be done quickly–in under 2 minutes–and still yields dramatic results. Making it part of your daily routine can greatly enhance your ability to feel positive emotions and will ensure your rapid recovery from depression and/or anxiety.

How to perform The Bow: Stand up with your feet about shoulder width. Bend your knees slightly. Make 2 fists and place them in the small of your back. Open your mouth as wide as possible and begin to lean backwards. This will be very uncomfortable, but it is one of the best ways to open up the energy channels of your body and release tension. When you perform this exercise, your whole body will begin to vibrate. This signifies the release of tension. Some people have so much tension that they don't experience the vibration until they practice the exercise a few times and learn to let go of resistance. While it is far better to have a trained therapist work with you on this, you can easily teach yourself and reap great benefits. Words are not entirely sufficient to describe this exercise, so I suggest that you google the phrase "Bioenergetic Bow Exercise" to get a physical demonstration and more info.

I cannot stress enough the importance of using the body to heal the mind. The two are actually one, so you must work with both if you want to see rapid results in your personal development program. Suppressed emotions are completely unconscious, so you cannot heal the pain of past traumas by working directly with the mind. Subconscious memories are actually stored in the musculature of the body, which explains why so many people today suffer from the inability to express themselves and feel happy. We tend to avoid our negative memories and emotions in hopes of forgetting them, but what many of us don't realize is that those memories are still very much a part of us. The only way to work through the pain of the past is to allow those repressed emotions to surface and be processed, and that is best done by working with the body, *not the mind*.

I'm confident that you now have enough information to begin some type of bioenergetic work. The two things I believe will help you the most are the use of a rebounder and daily practice of The Bow. These two tools alone have the potential to transform your life and put you on the path to extreme happiness and self-expression.

Now that you know how the body plays a huge role in your ability to be happy, let's explore how you can work directly with the mind to put yourself in an upward spiral of success and happiness.

Mental Programming and Positive Momentum

The mind is an incredible tool for navigating the world, but it also has many flaws. The mind is very easily influenced by its environment and subtle suggestions and images. One must be very careful when navigating the world and avoid getting trapped in a cycle of negativity. It's quite normal to experience extreme 'lows' in life, and it is always for our greatest good as long as we look at it as a learning lesson. Some people, however, become stuck in thoughts and feelings of apathy and self-pity. This keeps them trapped in negativity. Overcoming the negativity is only possible with a willingness to see things differently and seek help from others. You're doing great if you are reading this. It means you have kept an open mind and are willing to learn. I applaud you for that, and I am grateful for the opportunity to express my knowledge to you. I have overcome the depths of depression and severe anxiety, and I did it mostly through the reprogramming of my mind. I was so desperate that I was willing to do anything to turn my life around. My willingness to learn was what gave me the hope and inspiration to change. One thing I learned *a lot* about is the topic of mental programming and how to use my thoughts and emotions to create my reality. That is what this chapter is about, and I believe you will benefit greatly from using some of the following techniques.

The Power of Imagination

The most powerful tool that humans have been given is the faculty of imagination. No other animal on the planet has the ability to imagine scenarios before they happen (as far as we know). Imagination gives us the ability to project ourselves into the future and prepare accordingly. But I think imagination is much more than just a tool for preparation. I believe imagination is a *literal creator of circumstances and events*. I say this because I have consciously created many opportunities for myself with my imagination, and I have seen many others do the same thing. What would seem like 'lucky breaks' or 'coincidences' to the ordinary person are a regular occurrence in my life, and I am certain they are not just coincidences. I have been able to master my own thoughts and emotions to the point where I am able to manifest things in my life simply by focusing intensely on them. Everyone has this power but most are completely unaware of it and actually use it to their own detriment! For example, many people use their imagination to anticipate future events. But instead of thinking about things that excite and motivate them, they think about things that cause them worry and anxiety. The simple act of worrying about the possibility of failure actually increases the likelihood of failure, because imagination is a creative faculty of the mind, *not just something neat to play with*! It's time to start using your imagination wisely! When you master these techniques I am about to share with you, you will literally be able to create anything in your life that you truly desire. The mind is a *very* powerful thing. It's time to begin using it responsibly.

Even if you don't believe that you can literally create circumstances with your mind, I'd like you to just pretend that you can. Even if it's not true at all, it still serves you far better to take full responsibility for your life and not view yourself as a victim. In my study of successful people, I have yet to find one who doesn't believe that they create their own life with their own mind. Most of the people who live wonderful lives do so very consciously. They understand the power of their own thoughts and emotions, and they use them wisely to create the life they desire. It's important that you begin to use your mind intentionally as a tool for your own betterment. You can reach great heights, no matter where you happen to be right now, and I'm going to teach you how.

Your imagination is your greatest asset. With a little practice, you can begin to drastically alter the course of your life in whatever direction you choose. I'd like you to set aside about an hour of your time to do the following mental exercise. This technique has changed my life and countless others, and I want you to experience the incredible benefits that it offers as well.

The Perfect Day

First, you will need a notebook or a few sheets of paper and a pen. You're going to be planning out your ideal life on these sheets of paper, and they are going to help you make all your dreams come true. This really works wonders. It may be the most powerful personal development technique I have ever discovered. It is mind-blowing to see your life becoming exactly what you have envisioned. But like I said, the mind is a *very* powerful thing.

Before you write anything, I want you to take a few minutes to imagine your ideal life as vividly as possible. If you were living your wildest dreams and had no limits whatsoever, what would your life look like? Now, imagine that you had to live one day over and over again for the rest of your life. What would you do on that day? Who would you see? What would you spend your time on? Where would you live? What car would you drive? Think in as much detail as possible and try to actually imagine yourself living this amazing life. Spend some time on this until you come up with a very clear mental picture. You are already well on your way to greater things, but the next step is crucial.

Now that you have a clear picture in your mind of your ideal day, you will need to write down the description of it in extreme detail. This is your future you are planning, so don't be afraid to spend some time on this! It doesn't matter at all if you don't believe in your ability to live your dreams right now, but it is absolutely crucial that you do this writing exercise. Write down exactly what you would do on your ideal day from the time you wake up to the time you go to sleep. What would you eat for breakfast? Who would you eat it with? What would you talk about? What would your house look like? What would you see when you looked out your window? What kind of work would you do? What would your friends be like? What smells, tastes, and sights would you experience? There are no limits to this exercise. In fact, the more detailed you get, the more effective it will be and the faster you will attract these things into your life. You could get as specific as to mention the color of your bathroom tile or the shape of your bedroom window. Spend a considerable amount of time on this and fill up as many sheets of paper as you need to. You will want to thank me later!

Why is this exercise so powerful? It has to do with the reticular activating system of the brain. This part of the brain acts as a filtering system and causes you to recognize only the things that are most aligned with your own thinking. For example, you've probably had the experience of buying a new car and then suddenly you start noticing the same car everywhere you go. This is your reticular activating system in action. It filters out what's not important and focuses your attention on things that are most relevant. With this writing exercise, you are essentially programming your mind to notice things in your environment that help you to reach your goals. The idea behind it is that if you continue to visualize and think about your ideal life, you will slowly but surely begin to recognize and attract things into your life that help to move you closer to your goals. You will begin to meet people and find yourself in circumstances that are perfectly aligned with your goals. Things will begin to fall into place perfectly without you having to do anything more than visualize what you want. The phenomenon is actually quite mysterious and can't be fully explained, but it works every time! If you understand the law of attraction, then this should all make sense to you. If not, don't worry, because all you need to do is this writing exercise in order to see it in action and become a believer.

As I said, you must visualize what you want. That is why it is necessary for you to write out your ideal life in extreme detail. The detailed description allows your mind to form a clear picture. The clear picture should evoke a specific emotion within you. The more descriptive you get, the more positive emotion you will feel. The description of your ideal day should make you excited! If it doesn't, then you should use more detail or simply practice forming a clearer picture in your mind. This should be something fun for you to do. Treat it as an entertaining daydreaming exercise.

Once you have written down the full description of your ideal day, you should read it a minimum of once per day for at least a month. Also, get into the habit of visualizing your ideal day whenever you get the opportunity. Make it a habit to think about your ideal life all the time! The more you do, the faster your life will change. Also, the more positive emotions you can generate within you when thinking about your ideal life, the more effective the visualization exercise will be and the faster you will notice major changes happening. Strong emotion mixed with thought is a powerful combination. Get really good at daydreaming about the life of your dreams. This will often have an immediate impact on your mood. You will feel happier and be more hopeful, especially when you can remind yourself that all your dreams can indeed come true. Don't worry about any action steps. Simply visualize what you want and generate positive emotions to the best of your ability, and miracles will surely begin to happen. Have faith and know that this is true. Your dreams aren't as far away as you might believe.

Thoughts Become Reality

The only difference between someone who is depressed and someone who is happy is their thoughts. A depressed person will tend to think constantly about all the negative things in their life. They will even take positive things and try to put a negative spin on them! Happy people tend to look at everything in a more positive light. They take seemingly negative things and put a positive spin on them. You see, it's all about perception. Two people can look at the exact same situation and see two totally different things. One person might lose their job and see it as devastating, while another person can lose their job and see it as an opportunity to find a better one. There are really no 'good' or 'bad' events in the world. It is all a matter of perception. Sometimes suffering is required for growth.

For most of my life, I was an extremely negative person. I would look at my life and think of all the things I was unsatisfied with. The world looked like a scary and hostile place. I lived in fear. Today, however, I see the world as a beautiful place full of opportunity and excitement. I recognize my flaws but focus on my strengths. It took me years to transition from a negative mindset to a positive one, but it has made all the difference in my life. I went from severely depressed to extremely happy, and I can say with confidence that it is only a matter of perception and how you think that is the difference between happiness and misery. Let me give you a few tools and suggestions that will help you become an extremely happy person. The following are some of the things that have had the biggest impact on my perception and the way I view the world.

Affirmations For Subconscious Programming

The subconscious mind controls the way we behave in the world. We are mostly unaware of what goes on in our subconscious mind, but it shows itself in every aspect of our lives. We have been programmed since birth by our parents, friends, television, music, education, and everything in our environment. Most people really don't have a clue why they do the things they do. That's because their actions result from their unconscious programming. If you are currently unsatisfied with your life, then you need to work on reprogramming your subconscious mind so that you can get different results. The only way to consciously program your subconscious mind is through repetition. The repetition of certain statements and ideas coupled with emotion is an extremely effective tool for creating change in your life. These statements are often referred to as affirmations. Affirmations have played a huge role in turning my life around, and I believe that everyone should get into the habit of using them on a daily basis. There are a few things you need to know when using affirmations. Many people use them and see no results because they are not really using them correctly. I'm going to teach you a method that will cause you to see results very quickly.

First of all, it's important to understand that words themselves have very little power. The power comes from the ideas that the words represent and the emotions that they evoke within you. Therefore, it is important to choose affirmations that really make you feel good. A statement such as, "I am wealthy" is far less powerful than something like, "I am awakening to my true power and I will use this power to live my dreams and make a difference in the world." It will be different for each person, but a general rule when coming up with effective affirmations is to use statements that are specific and empowering. Use words that make you feel inspired and motivated. Your personal affirmations should be powerful enough to give you goosebumps all over your body. That's when you know they are working!

I have come up with a list of powerful affirmations that you may want to consider using. You can get them for free here, along with an audio version of them:

healthandhappinessfoundation.com/101-empowering-affirmations-for-success-confidence

This will save you a lot of time and effort, but I also encourage you to come up with your own affirmations as well. The more personal they are to you, the more effective they will be.

A lot of people find affirmations boring to use, so it can be very helpful to have them recorded on audio. With an audio recording, you can listen to affirmations passively throughout the day. Even if you are not paying attention to the words, the affirmations will reach your subconscious mind and have a direct effect on the way you think. This is especially true when the audio track has binaural beats playing in the background (included in the aforementioned article). Binaural frequencies actually change your brainwaves and allow the subconscious mind to be programmed much more easily. They are also relaxing and great to listen to while meditating.

Affirmations will impact you in a subtle way, but over time they will have a major impact. Remember, your subconscious mind contains many years of programming, so it will take a considerable amount of repetition for affirmations to have a noticeable impact on your attitude and perception. Every word counts though, so don't downplay the importance of using affirmations. Use them daily and you *will* see results. It may take a few months or even a few years, but that is irrelevant. The important thing is that you are changing for the better.

Incorporate affirmations in every way possible. Write them often, listen to them over and over again, speak them while looking at yourself in the mirror, paste them all over your house so you are forced to look at them, or do anything at all that you can think of to ensure you are always being bombarded with positive statements. What you put in your mind is what you get out. Put in positivity and you will have no choice but to live a positive and happy life.

Adopt the Beliefs of People You Wish to Be Like

There is a very easy way to achieve everything you desire. Simply find the people who are already living how you wish to live, and then *find out how they think*. If you can begin thinking like a successful and happy person, then you will inevitably become one yourself. This is why it is so important to have role models and to study the lives of people who are living their dreams. If you are depressed, then your current beliefs are not aligned with your dreams. Simply shifting your beliefs will have a profound impact on your life, and that can be done quite easily by learning about the beliefs of your role models. This is not so difficult when you consider that most of the successful people of the world have written books or have had books written about them. Reading about these people will help you to become like them. It is a well-known fact that all great leaders are readers. If you want to be successful and happy, self-education through reading is essential. Here are some of the best books I have ever read. These will help you greatly. If you don't enjoy reading, then you probably just need to read more (all taste is acquired), but you always have the option to listen to the audio version.

View my recommended reading material at the following web address:

healthandhappinessfoundation.com/ recommended-reading

Reading these books will help you shift your mindset to a more positive one. I attribute much of my happiness today to my habit of daily reading. When you read inspiring books, you adopt the ideas in the book almost by osmosis. The more you read and learn about what it takes to become extremely happy and successful, the better your chances are for becoming just that. You will begin to think differently, and as you do, you will see changes happening in your life. There is a law of the universe that requires everything to be in perfect balance, therefore, your external environment (circumstances, people, events) will always match your internal environment (thoughts and emotions). When you change the way you think, you change your entire life. It cannot be any other way.

Depression is a Blessing

You may not see it yet, but I promise you will one day very soon. Contrast is necessary for us to live the best lives possible. We need to know suffering in order to know joy. We become better people when we overcome our struggles, just like the roots of a tree grow stronger with the resistance of the wind. Embrace the struggle. Don't resist it. Face it like a champion and know that you will come out on top. Your struggle does not define you. Your ability to overcome it does.

I've talked to and studied many very successful people who thoroughly enjoy their lives, and every single one of them endured a severe depression or setback at some time in their life. People who never struggle never grow either. Consider yourself extremely blessed to be struggling, because you will conquer this and be much more resilient when it's over.

Each and every one of us are capable of living happy and fulfilling lives. You may be struggling now, but you will one day live blissfully if you simply take the time to apply the strategies in this book and continue to educate yourself. You will go far, my friend. I believe in you. Go get what you deserve and never let yourself settle for less. Love yourself. Remind yourself every day of how great you are. No one can tell you different, because YOU are the creator of your reality. It starts within. Now let that light of yours shine bright and show the world what you're made of.

Thank you so much for taking the time to read this book. I truly hope it helps you to start living the life you desire.

For more life-changing personal development tips, or to learn more about me, visit:

www.healthandhappinessfoundation.com

Other Resources:

My Youtube Channel:
BeauNorton.com

My Recommended Reading Material:
www.healthandhappinessfoundation.com/
recommended-reading

101 Affirmations on Audio w/ Binaural Beat Technology:
www.healthandhappinessfoundation.com/
101-affirmations-for-success-audio

Notes